ROHIT SHARMA COLOUR

INDIAN CRICKETER

MR VIVEK KUMAR PANDEY SHAMBHUNATH

ISBN 979-888530987-5

Short biography of Rohit Sharma and about life.During writing this book no character &
no religious are harmed written by Mr Vivek Kumar Pandey. winner youngest writer
award 1st rank in india 2020.He is only one writer can publish 700+ own book that was
greatest successfull in his life . This book fully colour edition books.

Contents

Foreword

Author biography in English :MY NAME IS VIVEK KUMAR PANDEY .
I WAS BORN IN 30 SEP 2002,I AM FROM SURAT GUJARAT INDIA.MY
DREAM WAS TO BE GOOD WRITERS ,MY FAMILY SUPPORTED ME
TO SUCCESSFUL AND I CAN DO IT MY SELF.How do I write? That
is a question, I believe, that cannot be honestly answered by
me."CELEBRATING YOUNGEST WRITER AWARD WINNER IN GUJARAT
1ST RANK" MR PANDEY JI . I may think I did a good job writing something
when in reality it could be horrible. The reader is the one who decides the
quality of my writing. I do not find writing to be natural to me and therefore
find it to be a real challenge. My trick as a challenged writer is to do the best
I can and know that I am happy with the final outcome. It may take a while
to do my best and there may be quite a few problems I run into along the
way.

I am not a greedy person those who are thinking about me and my
self I never tried it anyone people suffering from sadness ,I trying to get
promoted people suffering from happiness and joy in your Life Time. Now
in current situation in India and also world people are unemployed and have
no many but our indian governor help to people to get free food from ration
card , i also take part in leadership team ,i am Motivational speaker , Film
script writer. There was my two dream firstly writer and secondly actor &
also my own film is upcoming soon i done almost completely completed
script for my film .I AM GOING TO SAY WORD OF HEART TOUCH OUT
PLEASE READ IT" , firstly i thanks my father he supports me in this field
they always getting inspired me by own his words and behavior ,they always
said that he was a biggest person in the world in future and also they
purchase fruit and chocolate for me in anytime & anyway , firstly my father
buy him then call me Vivek you want a chocolate i will say yes papa but how
many tell me ,papa: you tell me how much i buy him i told 1 or 2 chocolate
but my father purchase whole the boxes of chocolate and they get suprised
me. MY FATHER WAS BORN IN " 20 SEPTEMBER" 1971 IN INDIA.

1) MY FATHER FAVORITE CLOTHES IS KURTA PAIJMA AND ALSO
STYLES SHOE

2) FAVORITE SINGER IS KISHORE DA

3) FAVORITE STATE GUJARAT AND KOLKATA , HIS VILLAGE IN
BIHAR

4) FAVORITE COLOR BLACK AND WHITE

THEY ALSO LOVE cricket like IPL and one day t-20 .they also like watching a News daily and heard the song daily ,they also interested in tik tok video but in current time tik tok is banned in india but also few videos are in you tube. In lockdown time my family and me very enjoy day daily. my father play daily ludo with his sister and son, daughter.they always loved tea and coffee anytime call me "। विवेक थोडा़ चाय बनाओना विवेक तुम्हारे हाथ का चाय अच्छा लगता है". I make it tea for my father but some reason after the April to june they are suffering from fever and cough , weakness on 6 June 2020 my father death. they not told me say bye bye his life. After death of 6 June on 10 june my mom and dad anniversary.but my father is Best in the world they can do anything for me please take care of father and respect it of your parents.

CHAPTER ONE

Rohit Sharma Colour

- Rohit Sharma

1. During writing this book no character & no religious are harmed written by Mr Vivek Kumar Pandey.

- Early life

Sharma was born on 30 April 1987 in Bansod, Nagpur, Maharashtra. His mother, Purnima Sharma, is from Visakhapatnam.His father, Gurunath Sharma, worked as a caretaker of a transport firm storehouse. Sharma was raised by his grandparents and uncles in Borivali because of his father's low income. He would visit his parents, who lived in a single-room house in Dombivli, only during weekends. He has a younger brother, Vishal Sharma.

Sharma joined a cricket camp in 1999 with his uncle's money. Dinesh Lad, his coach at the camp, asked him to change his school to Swami Vivekanand International School, where Lad was the coach and the cricket facilities were better than those at Sharma's old school. Sharma recollects, "I told him I couldn't afford it, but he got me a scholarship. So for four years I didn't pay a penny, and did well in my cricket". Sharma started as an off-spinner who could bat a bit before Lad noticed his batting ability and promoted him from number eight to open the innings. He excelled in the Harris and Giles Shield school cricket tournaments, scoring a century on debut as an opener.

- Youth and domestic first-class career

Sharma made his List A debut for West Zone against Central Zone in the Deodhar Trophy at Gwalior in March 2005. Batting at number eight, he scored 31 not out as West Zone won by 3 wickets with 24 balls remaining. Cheteshwar Pujara and Ravindra Jadeja made their debuts in the same match. It was Sharma's unbeaten innings of 142 in 123 balls against North Zone at the Maharanna Bhupal College Ground in Udaipur in the same tournament that brought him into the limelight. He visited Abu Dhabi and Australia with the India A squad and was then included among India's 30-member probables list for the upcoming ICC Champions Trophy tournament, although he did not make the final squad.

Sharma made his first-class debut for India A against New Zealand A at Darwin in July 2006. He scored 57 and 22 as India won by 3 wickets. He made his Ranji Trophy debut for Mumbai in the 2006–07 season and scored 205 off 267 balls against Gujarat. Mumbai went on to win the tournament with Sharma scoring a half-century (57) in his second innings in the final against Bengal.

Sharma has spent his entire domestic first-class career at Mumbai. In December 2009, he made his highest career score of 309 not out in the Ranji Trophy against Gujarat. In October 2013, upon the retirement of Ajit Agarkar, he was appointed team captain ahead of the 2013–14 season.

- International career

- Test matches

In November 2013, during Sachin Tendulkar's farewell series, Sharma made his Test debut at Eden Gardens in Kolkata against the West Indies and scored 177, the second-highest score on debut by an Indian to Shikhar Dhawan (187). He followed it up with 111 (not out) in the second Test at his home ground, the Wankhede Stadium in Mumbai.

Having been out of the Test team since 2017–18, Sharma went on the 2018–19 tour of Australia after he had earned a recall earlier. Chief selector M. S. K. Prasad said the reason for his recall was that his natural game suited the bouncy Australian pitches. Sharma played in the first Test in Adelaide, scoring 37 and 1 in an Indian victory. During the first Test, he sustained a minor injury which saw him miss the second Test in Perth. He recovered for the Boxing Day third Test at Melbourne and scored 63 (not out) to help India total 443/7 and win both the Test and the series. After the third Test,

Sharma had to return to India for the birth of his daughter.

In October 2019, in the third Test against South Africa, Sharma scored his 2,000th run and his first double century in Tests. He made 212 in the first innings of the match. Sharma was named as vice-captain of India's Test team during the tour of Australia in 2020, replacing Cheteshwar Pujara.

Sharma had a successful home series against England in 2021. Instrumental in his team's comeback after a defeat in the first Test at Chennai, he scored a century, one that The Guardian termed "deserves to be considered one of the greatest this century."He put on 167 runs with Ajinkya Rahane for the fourth wicket while making 161 runs in an innings that included 18 fours and two sixes. India went on to win the Test by 317 runs. He top-scored for his side in both innings of the low-scoring third Test in Ahmedabad with scores of 66 and 25 contributing to his team's win. He finished the series aggregating 345 runs, the most for India, at 58.

He scored his first overseas Test century on 4 September 2021 with an innings of 127 against England at The Oval, also reaching the target of 3,000 runs in Test cricket. Sharma and KL Rahul became the first opening pair to score more than 300 runs for India in a single Test series in England.

- 2015 and 2019 Cricket World Cups

- Sharma during the 2015 Cricket World Cup in Australia

In March 2015, Sharma made his first appearance in the Cricket World Cup and played in eight matches for India in the 2015 tournament in Australia. India reached the semi-final stage where they were defeated by Australia. Sharma scored 330 runs in the tournament with one century, a score of 137 in the quarter-final against Bangladesh.

On 15 April 2019, Sharma was appointed vice-captain of India's squad for the 2019 tournament in England. In the opening match against South Africa, he scored 122, including his 12,000th run in international cricket. In the match against Sri Lanka, he became the first batsman to score five centuries in the same World Cup tournament, and equalled Tendulkar's record for the most centuries in all World Cup matches. Sharma totalled 648 runs in the tournament to finish as the leading run-scorer and win the ICC's Golden Bat award, the third Indian player to do so.

- Other one-day international matches

Sharma made his full international debut in a one-day match against Ireland in Belfast on 23 June 2007. This was part of the 2007 Future Cup competition which also involved South Africa. He was number seven in the batting order but did not bat as India won the game by 9 wickets.

- He scored his maiden ODI half-century (52) against Pakistan at Jaipur on 18 November 2007 and was selected for the Indian squad going to the 2007–08 Commonwealth Bank Series in Australia In that series, he scored 235 runs at an average of 33.57 with 2 fifties, including 66 in the first final at Sydney when he partnered Sachin Tendulkar for most of India's successful run chase. After that, however, his ODI performances suffered a downturn and he lost his middle-order position to Suresh Raina. Later, Virat Kohli took his position as the reserve batsman. In December 2009, following his triple century in the Ranji Trophy, he was recalled to the ODI team for the tri-nations tournament in Bangladesh as Tendulkar opted to rest in the series.

He scored his maiden ODI century (114) against Zimbabwe on 28 May 2010 and followed it up with another century in the next match of the tri-series against Sri Lanka on 30 May 2010 by scoring 101 not out. He had a run of poor form in South Africa just before the 2011 World Cup and as a consequence he was left out of India's squad for the tournament.

- Sharma was recalled to the limited-overs squad for the tour of the West Indies in June and July 2011. In the first match at Queen's Park Oval, he scored 68 (not out) from 75 balls with three fours and a six. In the third match at the Sir Vivian Richards Stadium in Antigua, he scored a match-winning 86 off 91 balls after India had been reduced to 92 for 6.

He had a disastrous loss of form in 2012 and scored only 168 runs in the whole calendar year at the very low average of 12.92 with just a single half-century. Even so, his captain Mahendra Singh Dhoni showed faith in him, and his career was revived in 2013. Dhoni decided to move him up the batting order to open the innings with Shikhar Dhawan in the 2013 ICC Champions Trophy. The pairing was a success and India won the competition, defeating hosts England in the final.

His good form continued and, later in the year against Australia, he scored 141 (not out) in Jaipur. He followed that with 209 off 158 balls in

Bangalore and established a then-world record for the most sixes (16) in a one-day international innings (since beaten by Eoin Morgan of England with 17). On 13 November 2014, playing against Sri Lanka at Eden Gardens in Kolkata, Sharma broke the world record for the highest score in a one-day international innings with 264 from 173 deliveries.

In December 2017, India's captain Virat Kohli was rested for the series against Sri Lanka, in preparation for India's tour to South Africa, which began in the first week of January 2018. In his place, Sharma was appointed team captain and India under his leadership won the series 2–1, their eighth consecutive series win since defeating Zimbabwe in June 2016.

- In the year 2018, He led the team India to win ICC Asia Cup Finals against Bangladesh under his captaincy.

On 12 January 2019, in the opening match against Australia at the Sydney Cricket Ground, Sharma scored 133 but it was in vain as India lost by 34 runs. It was his 22nd century in one-day internationals. At Delhi on 13 March 2019, in the fifth and final match of a home series against Australia, Sharma scored 56 including his 8,000th run in one-day internationals. It was his 200th innings.] In 2019, he scored the most runs in ODIs by any batsman, with 1,490 runs in the year.

- Twenty20 international matches

- Sharma hitting a six

Sharma was included in the Indian squad for the 2007 ICC World Twenty20 and made his mark by scoring an unbeaten 50 from 40 deliveries against hosts South Africa in the quarter-finals. This enabled India to win the match by 37 runs and they went on to defeat Pakistan in the final, when Sharma scored 30 (not out) from 16 deliveries.

On 2 October 2015, during the South African tour of India, Sharma scored 106 in the first Twenty20 international at HPCA Stadium in Dharamshala. With that, he became the second Indian cricketer to have scored centuries in all three formats of international cricket. On 8 July 2018, during a series in England, Sharma became the second Indian batsman, after Virat Kohli, to score 2,000 runs in a Twenty20 international career. He was the fifth batsman worldwide to achieve the feat; the others besides Kohli were Brendon McCullum, Martin Guptill and Shoaib Malik.

- In 2018, He led the Team India to win the Nidahas Trophy under his captaincy

In November 2019, in the opening match of the series against Bangladesh, Sharma became the most-capped cricketer for India in T20Is, playing in his 99th match.In the next match of the series, he became the first male cricketer for India to play in 100 T20Is.

In November 2020, Sharma was nominated for the ICC Men's ODI and T20I Cricketer of the Decade awards. In September 2021, Sharma was named in India's squad for the 2021 ICC Men's T20 World Cup.

On 8 November 2021, Sharma scored his 3,000[th] run in T20Is and became the 3rd batsman to do so, He also became the 2nd Batsman to have scored 3,000 in all three formats of the game

- Indian Premier League

Sharma joined the Indian Premier League (IPL) in 2008 when he was signed by the Deccan Chargers franchise, based in Hyderabad, for the sum of US$750,000 a year. In the 2011 auction, he was sold for US$2 million to the Mumbai Indians.He scored his only IPL century in the 2012 tournament with 109 (not out) against the Kolkata Knight Riders. Under his leadership, Mumbai has won the IPL in 2013, 2015, 2017, 2019 and 2020; they also won the former Champions League Twenty20 competition in 2013.

Sharma has been one of the most successful players in the IPL as captain since 2013 of the Mumbai Indians, who have won the tournament five times under his leadership. He is currently (March 2021) one of four players who have scored 5,000 career runs in the competition. Sharma has 5,200+ runs with one century and 40 half centuries and is the fourth-highest run scorer after Virat Kohli, Suresh Raina and David Warner.

- Playing style

Sharma playing a late cut shot during the 2015 World Cup
Sharma is an aggressive batsman but with style and elegance. He is usually an opening batsman in limited-overs cricket but has played most of his Test cricket as a middle-order batsman.

Sunil Gavaskar considers Sharma to have a batting style similar to those of Virender Sehwag and Viv Richards. In his column for The Times of India in November 2018, Gavaskar said.

The standout performer in both the limited overs series and the T20 series has been Rohit Sharma. Like Virender Sehwag before him, he is unstoppable once he gets going and like Viru he has an appetite for big hundreds. When Viru used to get out looking to hit another delivery out of the park, there used to be consternation around the ground, just like it is when Rohit gets out to a seemingly casual shot. If Rohit can turn his white ball exploits into red ball cricket, he will be the most destructive batsman in the world after Viv Richards and Virender Sehwag.

While Sharma is not a regular bowler, he can bowl right arm off spin.He usually fields in the slips and says this is a part of his game on which he works very hard for improvement.

- Achievements

See also: List of highest individual scores in One Day International cricket

Sharma holds the world record for the highest individual score by a batsman playing in a one-day international match, having scored 264 against Sri Lanka at Eden Gardens, Kolkata, on 13 November 2014.He is the only player to have scored three double-centuries in this form of international cricket. In January 2020, Sharma was named as the ODI Player of the Year by the International Cricket Council (ICC).During the 2019 World Cup, Sharma became the only batsman to scored five centuries in a single edition of the Cricket World Cup.

On 5 October 2019, during a Test match against South Africa, Sharma became the first batsman to score two centuries in a match on his first appearance as an opening batsman. In the same series, he broke Shimron Hetmyer's record for the highest number of sixes in a Test series.

- National honours

1. Sharma receiving Arjuna award
2. 2015 – Arjuna Award
3. 2020 – Major Dhyan Chand Khel Ratna

- Sporting honours

1. ICC ODI Player of the Year: 2019

- Outside cricket

- Personal life

Sharma and Ritika Sajdeh during their wedding
Sharma married Ritika Sajdeh in December 2015. They have a daughter, born in December 2018.[

- Commercial endorsements

Sharma has been sponsored by several brands including CEAT and the Swiss watchmaker Hublot.In his career, Sharma has endorsed many other brands including Maggi, Fair and Lovely, Lay's, Nissan, energy drink Relentless, Nasivion nasal spray, Aristocrat by VIP Industries, Adidas and Oppo mobiles.

- Philanthropy

Sharma engages in numerous philanthropic activities, promoting various causes such as animal welfare, health, and children.He is particularly vocal about the protection of animals and has supported various initiatives and organisations to promote the cause.

In February 2015, Sharma joined People for the Ethical Treatment of Animals (PETA) to support sterilisation of homeless cats and dogs. When supporting the cause Sharma said, "Sterilisation is important because I feel that if we can stop (the homeless-animal crisis), there will be control of population among the street dogs".

- In September 2015, along with Hollywood actors Matt LeBlanc and Salma Hayek, Sharma joined an anti-poaching campaign in Kenya to save the wild animals of Africa including the last surviving northern white rhinoceros. When joining the campaign Sharma said, "I have been a member of PETA and when I was informed about the cause, I thought it is my duty to join the anti-poaching drive. That's what got me to Nairobi.

I was fascinated to have a look at Sudan (the last northern white rhino) and the sniffer dogs who catch hold of the poachers".

In November 2017, Sharma in a video on social media said that he had agreed with an online store to merchandise mobile phone covers and other items that would use his name and ODI jersey no. 45. Sharma also told his Twitter followers: "All proceeds from your purchases would go to an animal charity of my choice".

- In 2018 on "World Rhino Day", Sharma was announced as the WWF-India Rhino Ambassador. Ravi Singh, the CEO and Secretary General of WWF-India, said about the association with Sharma: "We are encouraged that sportsmen like Rohit are coming forward to support the call for conservation. Rohit's contribution to international cricket is well known and his supporting the conservation of rhinoceros in India will help the cause of the species. We welcome Rohit into the WWF family". After taking a pledge for the cause of rhino conservation, Sharma said, "My love for rhinos sparked when I first heard about Sudan, the last male northern white African rhino who passed away this year thus leading to the inevitable extinction of the entire species and that broke my heart. As the world and I mourned for my fallen friend Sudan, I researched the best way for me to help prevent something like this happening and the best way I know how is to create awareness. After getting in touch with WWF I learnt that 82% of the world's rhinos reside in India and I am honoured to be WWF-India's rhino ambassador to spread awareness and do my bit to contribute to the protection and survival of the rhino and help make this world a better place for them."

Sharma embraces heartfulness meditation. He laid the foundation stone for a cricket stadium in the presence of spiritual master Kamlesh D. Patel (known as Daaji) at the Heartfulness Institute in Hyderabad.

CHAPTER TWO

Let's Know About Cricket

- Cricket

Cricket is a bat-and-ball game played between two teams of eleven players on a field at the centre of which is a 22-yard (20-metre) pitch with a wicket at each end, each comprising two bails balanced on three stumps. The game proceeds when a player on the fielding team, called the bowler, "bowls" (propels) the ball from one end of the pitch towards the wicket at the other end. The batting side's players score runs by striking the bowled ball with a bat and running between the wickets, while the bowling side tries to prevent this by keeping the ball within the field and getting it to either wicket, and dismiss each batter (so they are "out"). Means of dismissal include being bowled, when the ball hits the stumps and dislodges the bails, and by the fielding side either catching a hit ball before it touches the ground, or hitting a wicket with the ball before a batter can cross the crease line in front of the wicket to complete a run. When ten batters have been dismissed, the innings ends and the teams swap roles. The game is adjudicated by two umpires, aided by a third umpire and match referee in international matches.

Forms of cricket range from Twenty20, with each team batting for a single innings of 20 overs and the game generally lasting three hours, to Test matches played over five days. Traditionally cricketers play in all-white kit, but in limited overs cricket they wear club or team colours. In addition to the basic kit, some players wear protective gear to prevent injury caused by the ball, which is a hard, solid spheroid made of compressed leather with a slightly raised sewn seam enclosing a cork core layered with tightly wound string.

The earliest reference to cricket is in South East England in the mid-16th century. It spread globally with the expansion of the British Empire, with the first international matches in the second half of the 19th century. The game's governing body is the International Cricket Council (ICC), which has over 100 members, twelve of which are full members who play Test matches. The game's rules, the Laws of Cricket, are maintained by Marylebone Cricket Club (MCC) in London. The sport is followed primarily in South Asia, Australasia, the United Kingdom, southern Africa and the West Indies.Women's cricket, which is organised and played separately, has also achieved international standard. The most successful side playing international cricket is Australia, which has won seven One Day International trophies, including five World Cups, more than any other country and has been the top-rated Test side more than any other country.

- History of cricket to 1725

A medieval "club ball" game involving an underhand bowl towards a batter. Ball catchers are shown positioning themselves to catch a ball. Detail from the Canticles of Holy Mary, 13th century.

Cricket is one of many games in the "club ball" sphere that basically involve hitting a ball with a hand-held implement; others include baseball (which shares many similarities with cricket, both belonging in the more specific bat-and-ball games category), golf, hockey, tennis, squash, badminton and table tennis. In cricket's case, a key difference is the existence of a solid target structure, the wicket (originally, it is thought, a "wicket gate" through which sheep were herded), that the batter must defend. The cricket historian Harry Altham identified three "groups" of "club ball" games: the "hockey group", in which the ball is driven to and fro between two targets (the goals); the "golf group", in which the ball is driven towards an undefended target (the hole); and the "cricket group", in which "the ball is aimed at a mark (the wicket) and driven away from it".

It is generally believed that cricket originated as a children's game in the south-eastern counties of England, sometime during the medieval period.Although there are claims for prior dates, the earliest definite reference to cricket being played comes from evidence given at a court case in Guildford in January 1597 (Old Style), equating to January 1598 in the modern calendar. The case concerned ownership of a certain plot of land and the court heard the testimony of a 59-year-old coroner, John Derrick, who gave witness that.

Being a scholler in the ffree schoole of Guldeford hee and diverse of his fellows did runne and play there at creckett and other plaies.

Given Derrick's age, it was about half a century earlier when he was at school and so it is certain that cricket was being played c. 1550 by boys in Surrey. The view that it was originally a children's game is reinforced by Randle Cotgrave's 1611 English-French dictionary in which he defined the noun "crosse" as "the crooked staff wherewith boys play at cricket" and the verb form "crosser" as "to play at cricket".

One possible source for the sport's name is the Old English word "cryce" (or "cricc") meaning a crutch or staff. In Samuel Johnson's Dictionary, he derived cricket from "cryce, Saxon, a stick". In Old French, the word "criquet" seems to have meant a kind of club or stick. Given the strong medieval trade connections between south-east England and the County of Flanders when the latter belonged to the Duchy of Burgundy, the name may have been derived from the Middle Dutch (in use in Flanders at the time) "krick"(-e), meaning a stick (crook). Another possible source is the Middle Dutch word "krickstoel", meaning a long low stool used for kneeling in church and which resembled the long low wicket with two stumps used in early cricket. According to Heiner Gillmeister, a European language expert of Bonn University, "cricket" derives from the Middle Dutch phrase for hockey, met de (krik ket)sen (i.e., "with the stick chase"). Gillmeister has suggested that not only the name but also the sport itself may be of Flemish origin.

- Growth of amateur and professional cricket in England

Evolution of the cricket bat. The original "hockey stick" (left) evolved into the straight bat from c. 1760 when pitched delivery bowling began.

Although the main object of the game has always been to score the most runs, the early form of cricket differed from the modern game in certain key technical aspects; the North American variant of cricket known as wicket retained many of these aspects. The ball was bowled underarm by the bowler and along the ground towards a batter armed with a bat that in shape resembled a hockey stick; the batter defended a low, two-stump wicket; and runs were called notches because the scorers recorded them by notching tally sticks.

In 1611, the year Cotgrave's dictionary was published, ecclesiastical court records at Sidlesham in Sussex state that two parishioners, Bartholomew Wyatt and Richard Latter, failed to attend church on Easter Sunday because they were playing cricket. They were fined 12d each and ordered to do penance.This is the earliest mention of adult participation in cricket and it was around the same time that the earliest known organised inter-parish or village match was played – at Chevening, Kent. In 1624, a player called Jasper Vinall died after he was accidentally struck on the head during a match between two parish teams in Sussex.

Cricket remained a low-key local pursuit for much of the 17th century. It is known, through numerous references found in the records of ecclesiastical court cases, to have been proscribed at times by the Puritans before and during the Commonwealth. The problem was nearly always the issue of Sunday play as the Puritans considered cricket to be "profane" if played on the Sabbath, especially if large crowds or gambling were involved.

According to the social historian Derek Birley, there was a "great upsurge of sport after the Restoration" in 1660. Gambling on sport became a problem significant enough for Parliament to pass the 1664 Gambling Act, limiting stakes to £100 which was, in any case, a colossal sum exceeding the annual income of 99% of the population. Along with prizefighting, horse racing and blood sports, cricket was perceived to be a gambling sport.Rich patrons made matches for high stakes, forming teams in which they engaged the first professional players.By the end of the century, cricket had developed into a major sport that was spreading throughout England and was already being taken abroad by English mariners and colonisers – the earliest reference to cricket overseas is dated 1676. A 1697 newspaper report survives of "a great cricket match" played in Sussex "for fifty guineas apiece" – this is the earliest known contest that is generally considered a First Class match.

- The patrons, and other players from the social class known as the "gentry", began to classify themselves as "amateurs" to establish a clear distinction from the professionals, who were invariably members of the working class, even to the point of having separate changing and dining facilities. The gentry, including such high-ranking nobles as the Dukes of Richmond, exerted their honour code of noblesse oblige to claim rights of leadership in any sporting contests they took part in, especially as it was necessary for them to play alongside their "social inferiors" if they were to win their bets. In time, a perception took hold that the typical amateur who played in first-class cricket, until 1962 when amateurism was abolished, was someone with a public school education who had then gone to one of Cambridge or Oxford University – society insisted that such people were "officers and gentlemen" whose destiny was to provide leadership. In a purely financial sense, the cricketing amateur would theoretically claim expenses for playing while his professional counterpart played under contract and was paid a wage or match fee; in practice, many amateurs claimed more than actual expenditure and the derisive term "shamateur" was coined to describe the practice.

- The Young Cricketer, 1768

The game underwent major development in the 18th century to become England's national sport.Its success was underwritten by the twin necessities of patronage and betting. Cricket was prominent in London as early as 1707 and, in the middle years of the century, large crowds flocked to matches on the Artillery Ground in Finsbury. The single wicket form of the sport attracted huge crowds and wagers to match, its popularity peaking in the 1748 season. Bowling underwent an evolution around 1760 when bowlers began to pitch the ball instead of rolling or skimming it towards the batter. This caused a revolution in bat design because, to deal with the bouncing ball, it was necessary to introduce the modern straight bat in place of the old "hockey stick" shape.

The Hambledon Club was founded in the 1760s and, for the next twenty years until the formation of Marylebone Cricket Club (MCC) and the opening of Lord's Old Ground in 1787, Hambledon was both the game's greatest club and its focal point. MCC quickly became the sport's premier club and the custodian of the Laws of Cricket. New Laws introduced in the latter part of the 18th century included the three stump wicket and leg before wicket (lbw).

The 19th century saw underarm bowling superseded by first roundarm and then overarm bowling. Both developments were controversial.Organisation of the game at county level led to the creation of the county clubs, starting with Sussex in 1839. In December 1889, the eight leading county clubs formed the official County Championship, which began in 1890.

The most famous player of the 19th century was W. G. Grace, who started his long and influential career in 1865. It was especially during the career of Grace that the distinction between amateurs and professionals became blurred by the existence of players like him who were nominally amateur but, in terms of their financial gain, de facto professional. Grace himself was said to have been paid more money for playing cricket than any professional.

The last two decades before the First World War have been called the "Golden Age of cricket". It is a nostalgic name prompted by the collective sense of loss resulting from the war, but the period did produce some great players and memorable matches, especially as organised competition at county and Test level developed.

- Cricket becomes an international sport

In 1844, the first-ever international match took place between the United States and Canada. In 1859, a team of English players went to North America on the first overseas tour. Meanwhile, the British Empire had been instrumental in spreading the game overseas and by the middle of the 19th century it had become well established in Australia, the Caribbean, India, Pakistan, New Zealand, North America and South Africa.

In 1862, an English team made the first tour of Australia. The first Australian team to travel overseas consisted of Aboriginal stockmen who toured England in 1868. The first One Day International match was played on 5 January 1971 between Australia and England at the Melbourne Cricket Ground.

In 1876–77, an England team took part in what was retrospectively recognised as the first-ever Test match at the Melbourne Cricket Ground against Australia. The rivalry between England and Australia gave birth to The Ashes in 1882, and this has remained Test cricket's most famous contest. Test cricket began to expand in 1888–89 when South Africa played England.

- World cricket in the 20th century

The inter-war years were dominated by Australia's Don Bradman, statistically the greatest Test batter of all time. Test cricket continued to expand during the 20th century with the addition of the West Indies (1928),

New Zealand (1930) and India (1932) before the Second World War and then Pakistan (1952), Sri Lanka (1982), Zimbabwe (1992), Bangladesh (2000), Ireland and Afghanistan (both 2018) in the post-war period. South Africa was banned from international cricket from 1970 to 1992 as part of the apartheid boycott.

- The rise of limited overs cricket

Cricket entered a new era in 1963 when English counties introduced the limited overs variant. As it was sure to produce a result, limited overs cricket was lucrative and the number of matches increased. The first Limited Overs International was played in 1971 and the governing International Cricket Council (ICC), seeing its potential, staged the first limited overs Cricket World Cup in 1975. In the 21st century, a new limited overs form, Twenty20, made an immediate impact. On 22 June 2017, Afghanistan and Ireland became the 11th and 12th ICC full members, enabling them to play Test cricket.

- A typical cricket field.

In cricket, the rules of the game are specified in a code called The Laws of Cricket (hereinafter called "the Laws") which has a global remit. There are 42 Laws (always written with a capital "L"). The earliest known version of the code was drafted in 1744 and, since 1788, it has been owned and maintained by its custodian, the Marylebone Cricket Club (MCC) in London.

- Playing area

Cricket is a bat-and-ball game played on a cricket field between two teams of eleven players each. The field is usually circular or oval in shape and the edge of the playing area is marked by a boundary, which may be a fence, part of the stands, a rope, a painted line or a combination of these; the boundary must if possible be marked along its entire length.

In the approximate centre of the field is a rectangular pitch (see image, below) on which a wooden target called a wicket is sited at each end; the wickets are placed 22 yards (20 m) apart. The pitch is a flat surface 10 feet (3.0 m) wide, with very short grass that tends to be worn away as the game progresses (cricket can also be played on artificial surfaces, notably matting). Each wicket is made of three wooden stumps topped by two bails.

• Cricket pitch and creases

As illustrated above, the pitch is marked at each end with four white painted lines: a bowling crease, a popping crease and two return creases. The three stumps are aligned centrally on the bowling crease, which is eight feet eight inches long. The popping crease is drawn four feet in front of the bowling crease and parallel to it; although it is drawn as a twelve-foot line (six feet either side of the wicket), it is, in fact, unlimited in length. The return creases are drawn at right angles to the popping crease so that they intersect the ends of the bowling crease; each return crease is drawn as an eight-foot line, so that it extends four feet behind the bowling crease, but is also, in fact, unlimited in length.

Before a match begins, the team captains (who are also players) toss a coin to decide which team will bat first and so take the first innings. Innings is the term used for each phase of play in the match.In each innings, one team bats, attempting to score runs, while the other team bowls and fields the ball, attempting to restrict the scoring and dismiss the batters. When the first innings ends, the teams change roles; there can be two to four innings depending upon the type of match. A match with four scheduled innings is played over three to five days; a match with two scheduled innings is usually completed in a single day. During an innings, all eleven members of the fielding team take the field, but usually only two members of the batting team are on the field at any given time. The exception to this is if a batter has any type of illness or injury restricting his or her ability to run, in this case the batter is allowed a runner who can run between the wickets when the batter hits a scoring run or runs,though this does not apply in international cricket. The order of batters is usually announced just before the match, but it can be varied.

The main objective of each team is to score more runs than their opponents but, in some forms of cricket, it is also necessary to dismiss all of the opposition batters in their final innings in order to win the match, which would otherwise be drawn. If the team batting last is all out having scored fewer runs than their opponents, they are said to have "lost by n runs" (where n is the difference between the aggregate number of runs scored by the teams). If the team that bats last scores enough runs to win, it is said to have "won by n wickets", where n is the number of wickets left to fall. For example, a team that passes its opponents' total having lost six wickets (i.e., six of their batters have been dismissed) have won the match "by four wickets".

In a two-innings-a-side match, one team's combined first and second innings total may be less than the other side's first innings total. The team with the greater score is then said to have "won by an innings and n runs", and does not need to bat again: n is the difference between the two teams' aggregate scores. If the team batting last is all out, and both sides have scored the same number of runs, then the match is a tie; this result is quite rare in matches of two innings a side with only 62 happening in first-class matches from the earliest known instance in 1741 until January 2017. In the traditional form of the game, if the time allotted for the match expires before either side can win, then the game is declared a draw.

If the match has only a single innings per side, then a maximum number of overs applies to each innings. Such a match is called a "limited overs" or "one-day" match, and the side scoring more runs wins regardless of the number of wickets lost, so that a draw cannot occur. In some cases, ties are broken by having each team bat for a one-over innings known as a Super Over; subsequent Super Overs may be played if the first Super Over ends in a tie. If this kind of match is temporarily interrupted by bad weather, then a complex mathematical formula, known as the Duckworth–Lewis–Stern method after its developers, is often used to recalculate a new target score. A one-day match can also be declared a "no-result" if fewer than a previously agreed number of overs have been bowled by either team, in circumstances that make normal resumption of play impossible; for example, wet weather.

In all forms of cricket, the umpires can abandon the match if bad light or rain makes it impossible to continue. There have been instances of entire matches, even Test matches scheduled to be played over five days, being lost to bad weather without a ball being bowled: for example, the third Test of the 1970/71 series in Australia.

• Innings

The innings (ending with 's' in both singular and plural form) is the term used for each phase of play during a match. Depending on the type of match being played, each team has either one or two innings. Sometimes all eleven members of the batting side take a turn to bat but, for various reasons, an innings can end before they have all done so. The innings terminates if the batting team is "all out", a term defined by the Laws: "at the fall of a wicket or the retirement of a batter, further balls remain to be bowled but no further batter is available to come in". In this situation, one of the batters has not been dismissed and is termed not out; this is because he has no partners left and there must always be two active batters while the innings is in progress.

- An innings may end early while there are still two not out batters

the batting team's captain may declare the innings closed even though some of his players have not had a turn to bat: this is a tactical decision by the captain, usually because he believes his team have scored sufficient runs and need time to dismiss the opposition in their innings

the set number of overs (i.e., in a limited overs match) have been bowled

the match has ended prematurely due to bad weather or running out of time

in the final innings of the match, the batting side has reached its target and won the game.

- Overs

The Laws state that, throughout an innings, "the ball shall be bowled from each end alternately in overs of 6 balls". The name "over" came about because the umpire calls "Over!" when six balls have been bowled. At this point, another bowler is deployed at the other end, and the fielding side changes ends while the batters do not. A bowler cannot bowl two successive overs, although a bowler can (and usually does) bowl alternate overs, from the same end, for several overs which are termed a "spell". The batters do not change ends at the end of the over, and so the one who was non-striker is now the striker and vice versa. The umpires also change positions so that the one who was at "square leg" now stands behind the wicket at the non-striker's end and vice versa.

- Clothing and equipment

English cricketer W. G. Grace "taking guard" in 1883. His pads and bat are very similar to those used today. The gloves have evolved somewhat. Many modern players use more defensive equipment than were available to Grace, most notably helmets and arm guards.

The wicket-keeper (a specialised fielder behind the batter) and the batters wear protective gear because of the hardness of the ball, which can be delivered at speeds of more than 145 kilometres per hour (90 mph) and presents a major health and safety concern. Protective clothing includes pads (designed to protect the knees and shins), batting gloves or wicket-keeper's gloves for the hands, a safety helmet for the head and a box for male players inside the trousers (to protect the crotch area). Some batters wear additional padding inside their shirts and trousers such as thigh pads, arm pads, rib protectors and shoulder pads. The only fielders allowed to wear protective gear are those in positions very close to the batter (i.e., if they are alongside or in front of him), but they cannot wear gloves or external leg guards.

Subject to certain variations, on-field clothing generally includes a collared shirt with short or long sleeves; long trousers; woolen pullover (if needed); cricket cap (for fielding) or a safety helmet; and spiked shoes or boots to increase traction. The kit is traditionally all white and this remains the case in Test and first-class cricket but, in limited overs cricket, team colours are worn instead.

- Bat and ball

Two types of cricket ball, both of the same size:
i) A used white ball. White balls are mainly used in limited overs cricket, especially in matches played at night, under floodlights (left).
ii) A used red ball. Red balls are used in Test cricket, first-class cricket and some other forms of cricket (right).
The essence of the sport is that a bowler delivers (i.e., bowls) the ball from his or her end of the pitch towards the batter who, armed with a bat, is "on strike" at the other end (see next sub-section: Basic gameplay).
The bat is made of wood, usually Salix alba (white willow), and has the shape of a blade topped by a cylindrical handle. The blade must not be more than 4.25 inches (10.8 cm) wide and the total length of the bat not more than 38 inches (97 cm). There is no standard for the weight, which is usually between 2 lb 7 oz and 3 lb (1.1 and 1.4 kg).

The ball is a hard leather-seamed spheroid, with a circumference of 9 inches (23 cm). The ball has a "seam": six rows of stitches attaching the leather shell of the ball to the string and cork interior. The seam on a new ball is prominent and helps the bowler propel it in a less predictable manner. During matches, the quality of the ball deteriorates to a point where it is no longer usable; during the course of this deterioration, its behaviour in flight will change and can influence the outcome of the match. Players will, therefore, attempt to modify the ball's behaviour by modifying its physical properties. Polishing the ball and wetting it with sweat or saliva is legal, even when the polishing is deliberately done on one side only to increase the ball's swing through the air, but the acts of rubbing other substances into the ball, scratching the surface or picking at the seam are illegal ball tampering.

- Player roles

Basic gameplay: bowler to batter
During normal play, thirteen players and two umpires are on the field. Two of the players are batters and the rest are all eleven members of the fielding team. The other nine players in the batting team are off the field in the pavilion. The image with overlay below shows what is happening when a ball is being bowled and which of the personnel are on or close to the pitch.

- Return crease

In the photo, the two batters (3 & 8; wearing yellow) have taken position at each end of the pitch (6). Three members of the fielding team (4, 10 & 11; wearing dark blue) are in shot. One of the two umpires (1; wearing white hat) is stationed behind the wicket (2) at the bowler's (4) end of the pitch. The bowler (4) is bowling the ball (5) from his end of the pitch to the batter at the other end who is called the "striker". The other batter (3) at the bowling end is called the "non-striker". The wicket-keeper (10), who is a specialist, is positioned behind the striker's wicket (9) and behind him stands one of the fielders in a position called "first slip" (11). While the bowler and the first slip are wearing conventional kit only, the two batters and the wicket-keeper are wearing protective gear including safety helmets, padded gloves and leg guards (pads).

While the umpire (1) in shot stands at the bowler's end of the pitch, his colleague stands in the outfield, usually in or near the fielding position called "square leg", so that he is in line with the popping crease (7) at the striker's end of the pitch. The bowling crease (not numbered) is the one on which the wicket is located between the return creases (12). The bowler (4) intends to hit the wicket (9) with the ball (5) or, at least, to prevent the striker (8) from scoring runs. The striker (8) intends, by using his bat, to defend his wicket and, if possible, to hit the ball away from the pitch in order to score runs.

Some players are skilled in both batting and bowling, or as either or these as well as wicket-keeping, so are termed all-rounders. Bowlers are classified according to their style, generally as fast bowlers, seam bowlers or spinners. Batters are classified according to whether they are right-handed or left-handed.

• Fielding

Of the eleven fielders, three are in shot in the image above. The other eight are elsewhere on the field, their positions determined on a tactical basis by the captain or the bowler. Fielders often change position between deliveries, again as directed by the captain or bowler.

If a fielder is injured or becomes ill during a match, a substitute is allowed to field instead of him, but the substitute cannot bowl or act as a captain, except in the case of concussion substitutes in international cricket. The substitute leaves the field when the injured player is fit to return. The Laws of Cricket were updated in 2017 to allow substitutes to act as wicket-keepers.

• Bowling and dismissal

Glenn McGrath of Australia holds the world record for most wickets in the Cricket World Cup.

Most bowlers are considered specialists in that they are selected for the team because of their skill as a bowler, although some are all-rounders and even specialist batters bowl occasionally. The specialists bowl several times during an innings but may not bowl two overs consecutively. If the captain wants a bowler to "change ends", another bowler must temporarily fill in so that the change is not immediate.

A bowler reaches his delivery stride by means of a "run-up" and an over is deemed to have begun when the bowler starts his run-up for the first delivery of that over, the ball then being "in play".

Fast bowlers, needing momentum, take a lengthy run up while bowlers with a slow delivery take no more than a couple of steps before bowling. The fastest bowlers can deliver the ball at a speed of over 145 kilometres per hour (90 mph) and they sometimes rely on sheer speed to try to defeat the batter, who is forced to react very quickly.

Other fast bowlers rely on a mixture of speed and guile by making the ball seam or swing (i.e. curve) in flight. This type of delivery can deceive a batter into miscuing his shot, for example, so that the ball just touches the edge of the bat and can then be "caught behind" by the wicket-keeper or a slip fielder. At the other end of the bowling scale is the spin bowler who bowls at a relatively slow pace and relies entirely on guile to deceive the batter. A spinner will often "buy his wicket" by "tossing one up" (in a slower, steeper parabolic path) to lure the batter into making a poor shot. The batter has to be very wary of such deliveries as they are often "flighted" or spun so that the ball will not behave quite as he expects and he could be "trapped" into getting himself out. In between the pacemen and the spinners are the medium paced seamers who rely on persistent accuracy to try to contain the rate of scoring and wear down the batter's concentration.

There are nine ways in which a batter can be dismissed: five relatively common and four extremely rare. The common forms of dismissal are bowled, caught, leg before wicket (lbw), run out and stumped. Rare methods are hit wicket,hit the ball twice, obstructing the field and timed out. The Laws state that the fielding team, usually the bowler in practice, must appeal for a dismissal before the umpire can give his decision. If the batter is out, the umpire raises a forefinger and says "Out!"; otherwise, he will shake his head and say "Not out".There is, effectively, a tenth method of dismissal, retired out, which is not an on-field dismissal as such but rather a retrospective one for which no fielder is credited.

• Batting, runs and extras

The directions in which a right-handed batter, facing down the page, intends to send the ball when playing various cricketing shots. The diagram for a left-handed batter is a mirror image of this one.

Batters take turns to bat via a batting order which is decided beforehand by the team captain and presented to the umpires, though the order remains flexible when the captain officially nominates the team. Substitute batters are generally not allowed, except in the case of concussion substitutes in international cricket.

In order to begin batting the batter first adopts a batting stance. Standardly, this involves adopting a slight crouch with the feet pointing across the front of the wicket, looking in the direction of the bowler, and holding the bat so it passes over the feet and so its tip can rest on the ground near to the toes of the back foot.

A skilled batter can use a wide array of "shots" or "strokes" in both defensive and attacking mode. The idea is to hit the ball to the best effect with the flat surface of the bat's blade. If the ball touches the side of the bat it is called an "edge". The batter does not have to play a shot and can allow the ball to go through to the wicketkeeper. Equally, he does not have to attempt a run when he hits the ball with his bat. Batters do not always seek to hit the ball as hard as possible, and a good player can score runs just by making a deft stroke with a turn of the wrists or by simply "blocking" the ball but directing it away from fielders so that he has time to take a run. A wide variety of shots are played, the batter's repertoire including strokes named according to the style of swing and the direction aimed: e.g., "cut", "drive", "hook", "pull".

The batter on strike (i.e. the "striker") must prevent the ball hitting the wicket, and try to score runs by hitting the ball with his bat so that he and his partner have time to run from one end of the pitch to the other before the fielding side can return the ball. To register a run, both runners must touch the ground behind the popping crease with either their bats or their bodies (the batters carry their bats as they run). Each completed run increments the score of both the team and the striker.

- Sachin Tendulkar is the only player to have scored one hundred international centuries

The decision to attempt a run is ideally made by the batter who has the better view of the ball's progress, and this is communicated by calling: usually "yes", "no" or "wait". More than one run can be scored from a single hit: hits worth one to three runs are common, but the size of the field is such that it is usually difficult to run four or more. To compensate for this, hits that reach the boundary of the field are automatically awarded four runs if the ball touches the ground en route to the boundary or six runs if the ball clears the boundary without touching the ground within the boundary. In these cases the batters do not need to run. Hits for five are unusual and generally rely on the help of "overthrows" by a fielder returning the ball. If an odd number of runs is scored by the striker, the two batters have changed ends, and the one who was non-striker is now the striker. Only the striker can score individual runs, but all runs are added to the team's total.

Additional runs can be gained by the batting team as extras (called "sundries" in Australia) due to errors made by the fielding side. This is achieved in four ways: no-ball, a penalty of one extra conceded by the bowler if he breaks the rules; wide, a penalty of one extra conceded by the bowler if he bowls so that the ball is out of the batter's reach bye, an extra awarded if the batter misses the ball and it goes past the wicket-keeper and gives the batters time to run in the conventional way leg bye, as for a bye except that the ball has hit the batter's body, though not his bat. If the bowler has conceded a no-ball or a wide, his team incurs an additional penalty because that ball (i.e., delivery) has to be bowled again and hence the batting side has the opportunity to score more runs from this extra ball.

- Specialist roles

Captain (cricket) and Wicket-keeper
The captain is often the most experienced player in the team, certainly the most tactically astute, and can possess any of the main skillsets as a batter, a bowler or a wicket-keeper. Within the Laws, the captain has certain responsibilities in terms of nominating his players to the umpires before the match and ensuring that his players conduct themselves "within the spirit and traditions of the game as well as within the Laws".

The wicket-keeper (sometimes called simply the "keeper") is a specialist fielder subject to various rules within the Laws about his equipment and demeanour. He is the only member of the fielding side who can effect a stumping and is the only one permitted to wear gloves and external leg guards. Depending on their primary skills, the other ten players in the team tend to be classified as specialist batters or specialist bowlers. Generally, a team will include five or six specialist batters and four or five specialist bowlers, plus the wicket-keeper.

- Umpires and scorers

Umpire (cricket), Scoring (cricket), and Cricket statistics
An umpire signals a decision to the scorers
The game on the field is regulated by the two umpires, one of whom stands behind the wicket at the bowler's end, the other in a position called "square leg" which is about 15–20 metres away from the batter on strike and in line with the popping crease on which he is taking guard. The umpires have several responsibilities including adjudication on whether a ball has been correctly bowled (i.e., not a no-ball or a wide); when a run is scored; whether a batter is out (the fielding side must first appeal to the umpire, usually with the phrase "How's that?" or "Owzat?"); when intervals start and end; and the suitability of the pitch, field and weather for playing the game. The umpires are authorised to interrupt or even abandon a match due to circumstances likely to endanger the players, such as a damp pitch or deterioration of the light.

Off the field in televised matches, there is usually a third umpire who can make decisions on certain incidents with the aid of video evidence. The third umpire is mandatory under the playing conditions for Test and Limited Overs International matches played between two ICC full member countries. These matches also have a match referee whose job is to ensure that play is within the Laws and the spirit of the game.

The match details, including runs and dismissals, are recorded by two official scorers, one representing each team. The scorers are directed by the hand signals of an umpire . For example, the umpire raises a forefinger to signal that the batter is out (has been dismissed); he raises both arms above his head if the batter has hit the ball for six runs. The scorers are required by the Laws to record all runs scored, wickets taken and overs bowled; in practice, they also note significant amounts of additional data relating to the game.

A match's statistics are summarised on a scorecard. Prior to the popularisation of scorecards, most scoring was done by men sitting on vantage points cuttings notches on tally sticks and runs were originally called notches.According to Rowland Bowen, the earliest known scorecard templates were introduced in 1776 by T. Pratt of Sevenoaks and soon came into general use.It is believed that scorecards were printed and sold at Lord's for the first time in 1846.

- thank you for buy & read this book

have a great day of your
from : Mr Vivek Kumar Pandey

www.ingramcontent.com/pod-product-compliance
Lightning Source LLC
Chambersburg PA
CBHW070327160726
47999CB00003B/1195